BRAIN GAMES®

ENERGY SCIENCE EXPERIMENTS

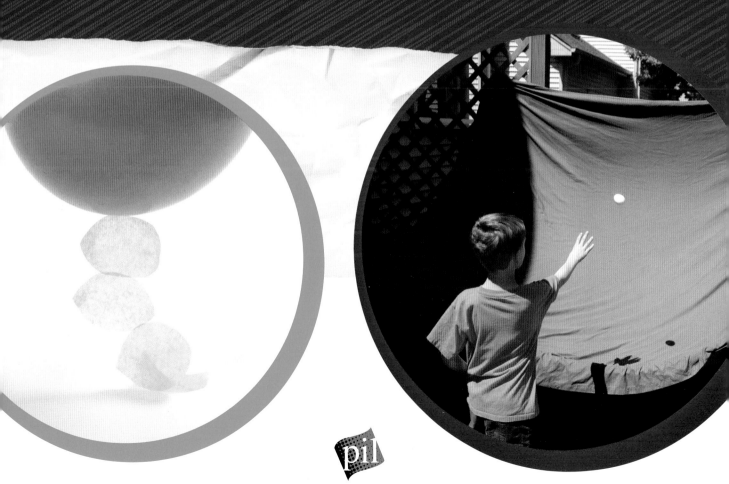

pil

Publications International, Ltd.

Written by Nicole Sulgit and Beth Taylor with additional material from Adam Parrilli
Photo styling by Nick LaShure, Ashley Joyce, and Nicole Sulgit
Photography by Christopher Hiltz, Nick LaShure and Nicole Sulgit
Additional images from Shutterstock.com

Louis Weber, CEO
Publications International, Ltd.
8140 Lehigh Avenue
Morton Grove, IL 60053

ISBN: 978-1-64558-523-7

Manufactured in China.

8 7 6 5 4 3 2 1

SAFETY WARNING

All of the experiments and activities in this book MUST be performed with adult supervision. All projects contain a degree of risk, so carefully read all instructions before you begin and make sure that you have safety materials such as goggles, gloves, etc. Also make sure that you have safety equipment, such as a fire extinguisher and first aid kit, on hand. You are assuming the risk of any injury by conducting these activities and experiments. Publications International, Ltd. will not be liable for any injury or property damage.

Let's get social!

@Publications_International

@PublicationsInternational

@BrainGames.TM

www.pilbooks.com

CONTENTS

INTRODUCTION

Heat energy from the sun, sound energy from people's voices, electrical energy that lights up our houses...energy and other forces like gravity surround us and affect us every day. In this book, you'll find out through experimentation more about how the world around us works.

PHYSICS

Physics is a branch of science that studies matter, energy, and the fundamental forces of the universe. Math and physics are closely tied together. As Isaac Newton was studying how motion, gravity, and force worked, he also was advancing the field of modern calculus, a branch of mathematics that studies change over a period of time.

ENERGY

In science, energy is the ability to do work. Sometimes energy is stored to be used later. This is called potential energy. When an object is moving, it is using kinetic energy.

An arrow about to be released has potential energy. An arrow in motion has kinetic energy.

MANY KINDS OF ENERGY

There are many kinds of energy, including heat energy, light energy, chemical energy that comes from chemical reactions, and electrical energy. Some sources of energy are renewable. For example, we can keep harnessing solar energy from the Sun. Other sources of energy are not renewable. Think of a campfire. You use wood to generate light and heat. But once a piece of wood is burned, it cannot be used again.

THREE LAWS OF MOTION

Sometimes if we watch an object move—a ball bouncing downhill—it seems random. But objects in motion follow certain rules. In the 1600s, Sir Isaac Newton described three laws of motion.

FIRST LAW OF MOTION

The first law says that an object at rest remains at rest, while an object in motion stays in motion, with the same direction and speed. Let's say a ball is sitting on the ground. Unless someone exerts a force on it by kicking it or pushing it, or a wind exerts a force on it to move it, the ball will stay on the ground. It won't just spontaneously fly in midair. If you roll a ball along the ground, it will keep going in the direction you rolled it. If it does change direction, it will be because of an outside force, like a bump in the ground. When it slows down, it will be because of the outside force of gravity, and other forces like friction from the carpeting.

SECOND LAW OF MOTION

The second law of motion says that objects with a larger mass require more force to move them. There is an equation that says Force = mass times acceleration.

THIRD LAW OF MOTION

The third law of motion says that for every action, there is an equal and opposite reaction. When you push on a wall, you are exerting a force on it. But the wall is also exerting a force in the opposite direction!

FRICTION

One of the forces that acts on a moving object is friction. When you roll a ball, it will eventually come to a halt because of friction. Some materials cause more friction than others. A wet floor provides less friction than a dry one!

CRAFT STICK BOMBS

Weave craft sticks together to create stick bombs. Then find out what happens when kinetic energy is released.

TRIANGLE BOMB

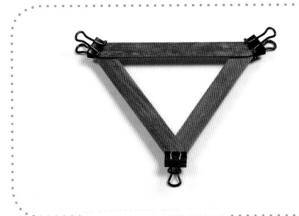

Step 1

Arrange 3 craft sticks in an upside-down triangle as shown. Add small binder clips where the sticks meet.

MATERIALS

- Jumbo craft sticks
- Small binder clips

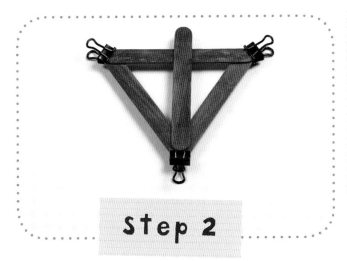

Step 2

Place another stick on top of the upside-down triangle in the middle.

Step 3

Weave the final stick under one side of the triangle, over the middle stick, and then under the other side of the triangle.

Step 4

Carefully remove the small binder clips to complete the triangle bomb. Tension will hold the stick bomb together until it hits something and the kinetic energy is released.

Step 5

In an empty area, throw your triangle bomb on the floor or another surface and watch it explode!

SQUARE BOMB

Step 1

Arrange 2 craft sticks in a T shape as shown with the middle stick under the top stick. Add a small binder clip where the sticks meet.

Step 2

Place 2 sticks on the sides, parallel with the middle stick, and overlapping the top stick. Add small binder clips where sticks meet.

Step 3

In the middle of the square you are creating, weave a stick over a side stick, under the middle stick, and then over the other side stick.

Step 4

At the bottom of the square you are creating, weave a stick under a side stick, over the middle stick, and then under the other side stick.

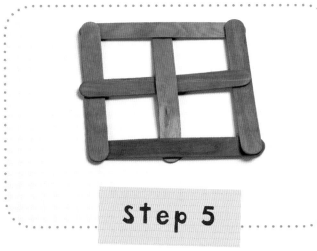

Step 5

Carefully remove the binder clips to complete the square bomb.

HOW DOES IT WORK?

Craft stick bombs are held together under tension. You create the tension by weaving the sticks together. These interwoven sticks can store a surprising amount of potential energy. When one key stick is dislodged, the energy is released, causing the entire stick bomb to explode into pieces.

EGGS-PERIMENT

An egg thrown directly at a wall will break. An egg thrown at a curved sheet stands a better chance. The sheet slows down the motion of the egg so that there is less of an impact. A car's airbags work on the same principles.

MATERIALS

- A sheet
- Two chairs
- Eggs
- Tape

Step 1

Attach a sheet on both sides to trees or posts. Do not tape it to a wall.

Step 2

Attach the bottom corners to two chairs. The sheet should form a slope.

Step 3

Grab some eggs. (Make sure to wash your hands after handling raw eggs.)

Step 4

Throw them at the sheet!

They don't break! Why not? If you threw an egg straight at a wall, it would break. But the sheet slows down the egg's motion over a longer period of time.

SEAT BELTS
AND AIRBAGS

People who design cars need to pay a lot of attention to safety. Remember how Newton's first law of motion said that an object in motion remains in motion? If a car stops abruptly, but the person inside it keeps moving forward at the same speed they were previously, that person will be hurt.

SEAT BELTS

Seat belts exert a force on the person in the car that opposes the force of them moving forward. The first cars didn't have seat belts, which were introduced in the 1940s and 1950s. In the United States, a law called the National Traffic and Motor Vehicle Safety Act passed in 1966. It created a Highway Safety Bureau that set safety standards that auto manufacturers had to follow. The implementation of seat belts, among other safety features such as shatterproof windshields, followed. However, many people still did not wear seat belts, until states began to pass laws in the 1980s and 1990s.

BOOSTER SEATS

Seat belts are designed for adults. Booster seats help seat belts fall in the right place, so that they will restrain without causing injury to a kid's neck or stomach.

AIRBAGS

With airbags, the time it takes for the person to stop moving increases; this reduces the amount of force involved. Airbags provide a cushion between the person and the steering wheel and dashboard.

The first airbag for an automobile was patented in the 1950s, but they weren't implemented until the 1970s, and they didn't become common until the 1990s.

RUBBER BAND SLINGSHOT

Turn potential energy into kinetic energy with a simple slingshot.

MATERIALS

- Two rubber bands
- Tape
- Paper or other soft material to propel with your slingshot

Safety note

Make sure you do not use hard material in your slingshot. Make sure anyone in the room is behind the slingshot when you use it.

Step 1

Put the two rubber bands so that they overlap slightly.

Step 2

Draw the rubber band on the right over the other rubber band, then underneath it and through the rubber band, to form a knot.

Step 3

Cut a length of tape to use as the cradle.

Step 4

Wrap the tape around the rubber band as a cradle.

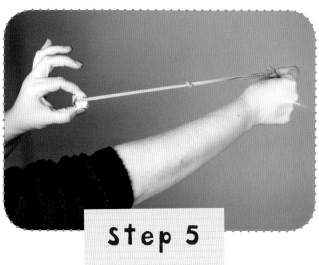

Step 5

Crumple up a ball of paper or a napkin and place it in the cradle. Pinch the paper in one hand while stretching the other end of the slingshot with your other hand.

Step 6

Release the slingshot! The paper ball goes flying.

EXPERIMENT MORE!

Experiment with the angle of your slingshot. What works best—for your hands to be level, or for one to be higher than the other? How does stretching the rubber band or using different sizes of rubber bands affect the experiment? How high can you shoot the paper ball? How far can you shoot it?

BALLOON ROCKET

Explore the physics behind thrust as you launch a balloon rocket.

MATERIALS

- Balloon
- Plastic straw
- 10-foot length of string
- 2 chairs
- Scissors
- Tape
- Small binder clip
- Ruler or measuring tape

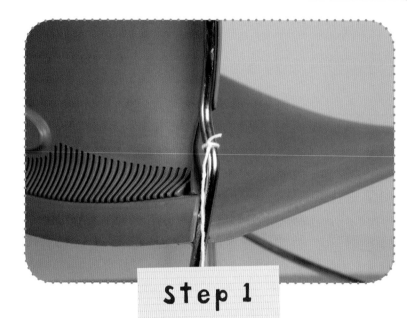

Step 1

Position chairs about 6–8 feet (1.8–2.4 m) apart with clear space in between. Tie one end of the string to one of the chairs.

Step 2

Cut a piece of straw approximately 2 inches (5 cm) long. Run the free end of the string through the piece of straw.

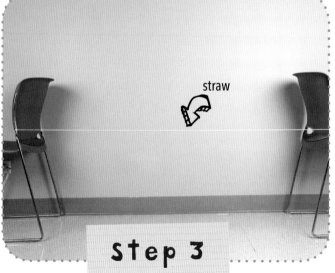

straw

Step 3

Pull the string going through the straw tight and tie the free end to the other chair.

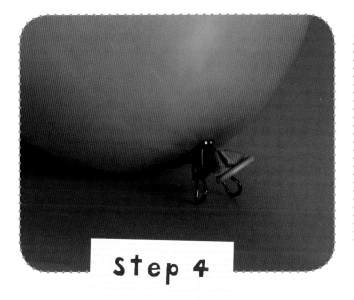

Step 4

Step 5

Inflate the balloon, but don't tie it off.
Twist the neck of the balloon and then clip it with a small binder clip so that no air escapes.

Tape the balloon to the straw so that the closed neck faces towards one of the chairs.

Step 6

Step 7

Pull the balloon to one end of the string so that its closed neck is close to that chair. *What do you think will happen when you release the balloon?*

Release the balloon's closed neck and watch it speed down its launch path!

HOW DOES IT WORK?

Your balloon rocket works thanks to thrust. When you inflated the balloon, you pushed air into it. When you released the closed neck, the air rushing out of the balloon created forward motion called thrust. Thrust is the pushing force that moved your balloon rocket along its launch path. In a real rocket launch, thrust is created by the force of burning rocket fuel as it blasts from the rocket's engine. As the engines blast down, the rocket goes up.

CONFETTI CANNON

Make a fun party favor with just a balloon, tape, and a toilet paper tube!

MATERIALS

- Toilet paper tube
- Balloon
- Scissors
- Masking tape or painter's tape
- Large pieces of confetti

Potential vs. Kinetic

This experiment is a great example of the transformation of potential energy (when you are holding the end of the balloon) to kinetic energy (when you release the balloon). The confetti is propelled into the air by that energy.

Step 1

Tie a knot at the end of the balloon.

Step 2

Cut off the top of the balloon. Cut off enough that the balloon will fit comfortably over the toilet paper tube.

Step 3

Fit the balloon over one end of the toilet paper tube.

Step 4

Tape the balloon to the tube with a strong tape such as masking tape.

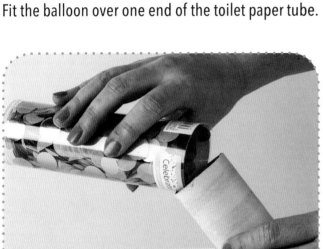

Step 5

Pour some confetti into the open end of the tube. Let it fall into the balloon. Don't use so much confetti that it clogs the tube.

Step 6

Pull down the end of the balloon.

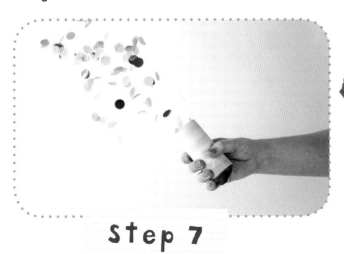

Step 7

Release the balloon. Confetti everywhere!

The party favor is re-usable—you can load it up with confetti and run the experiment again. Try a few different variations: use something heavier than confetti such as small fabric pompoms. Try more or less confetti—does the amount of confetti in the tube affect how far it goes? Does the amount you stretch the balloon in step 6 affect the amount of confetti released or how far it goes?

WINDMILLS

People harness energy from the wind through windmills and wind turbines. Windmills have been around for centuries. In older days, the wind would turn the blades, which would set other parts of the windmill in motion in order to grind flour, for example. Today, wind power can be transformed into electrical power.

Windmills and wind turbines are forms of renewable energy.

The Netherlands is known for its iconic windmills. They were used to pump water from farmlands prone to flooding.

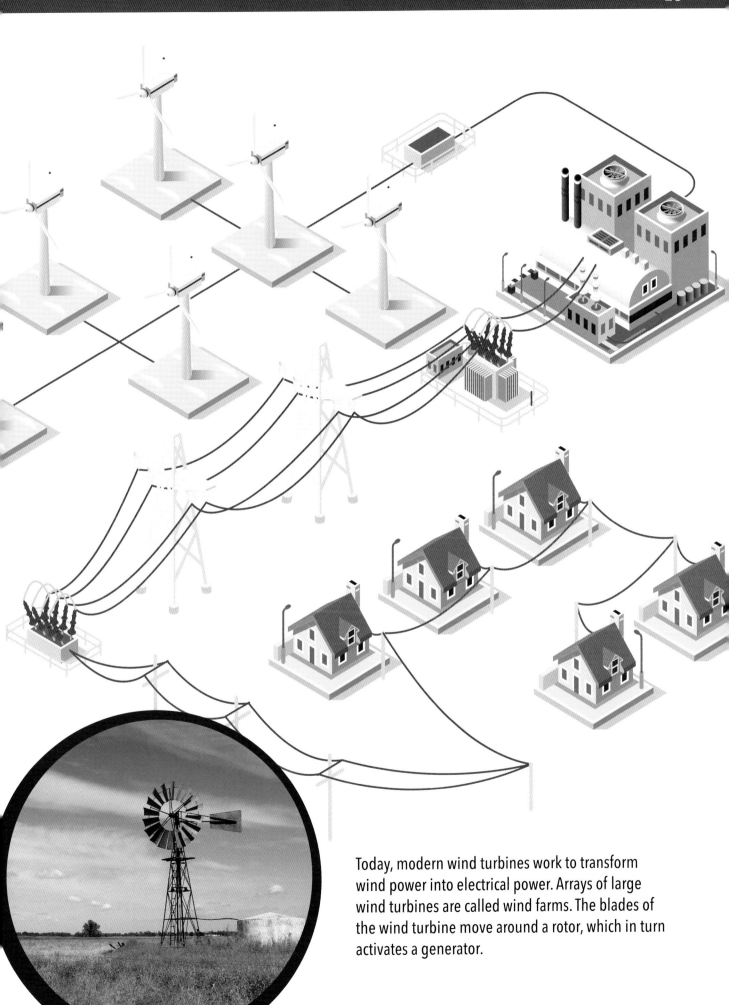

Today, modern wind turbines work to transform wind power into electrical power. Arrays of large wind turbines are called wind farms. The blades of the wind turbine move around a rotor, which in turn activates a generator.

WINDMILL

Make your own windmill model to see how it works.

MATERIALS

- 1 large plastic cup
- 2 small plastic cups
- 2 toilet paper cardboard tubes
- Cardboard
- Glue
- Painter's tape
- String or thread
- Small object such as a paper clip or safety pin
- Chopstick or skewer
- Adhesive putty

Step 1

Poke holes in the bottom of each paper cup.

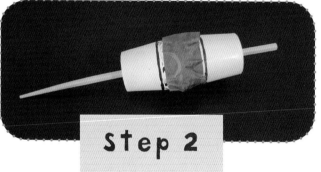

Step 2

Tape the cups together, facing each other. Poke the skewer through them.

Step 3

Tape the cups to the larger plastic cup that will act as your windmill base.

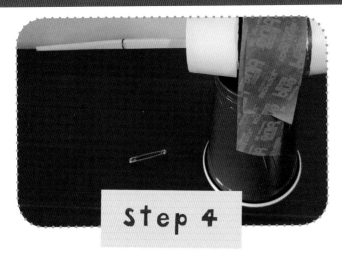

Step 4

Secure your paper clip or safety pin to one end of the skewer with string. It will be the load you are trying to lift.

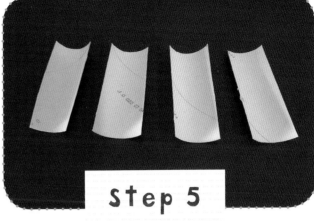

Step 5

Cut the toilet paper tubes to make four slightly curved blades.

Step 6

Cut two long strips from the cardboard and glue them to the blades.

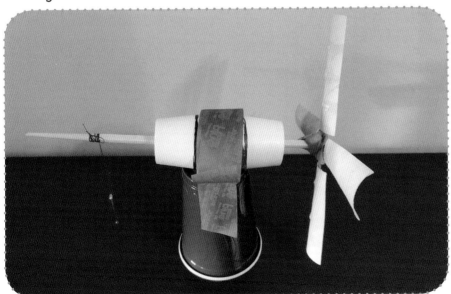

Step 7

Secure the blades to the end of the skewer with adhesive putty.

Step 8

Turn the blades. As you do, see how the skewer turns, lifting the safety pin off the ground.

SOLAR DISTILLER

Solar energy can be used to purify water. Wait for a hot, sunny day to perform this experiment.

MATERIALS

- 1 cup of water
- 1 tablespoon of salt
- Food coloring
- Large bowl
- Small bowl
- Plastic wrap
- Small stone

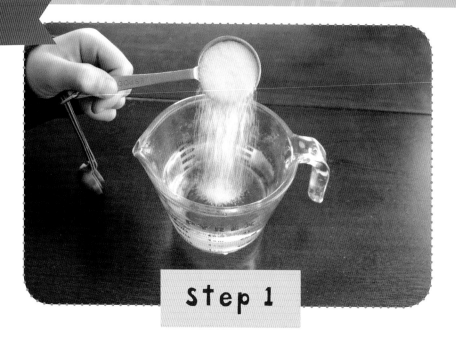

Step 1

Pour salt into the water to act as a contaminant.

Step 2

Mix the water and salt until it is cloudy.

Step 3

If desired, add some food coloring.

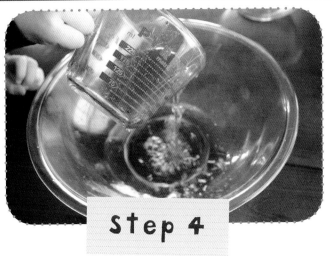

step 4

Pour the mixture into the large bowl.

step 5

Place the small bowl into the large bowl.

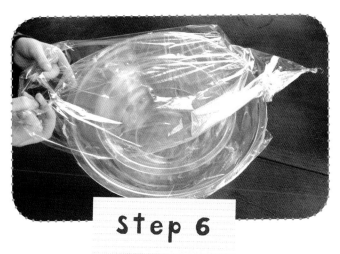

Step 6

Cover the bowls with plastic wrap.

Step 7

Place a stone or other small weight on the wrap.

Step 8

Leave the bowl in direct sunlight. You will begin to notice condensation gathering on the plastic wrap and dripping into the small bowl.

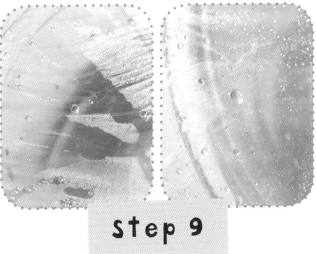

step 9

Energy from the sun heats the water. It evaporates, and then condenses on the plastic wrap. When it drips into the small bowl, it is free of salt.

SOUND

Sound is a kind of energy that moves in waves. Sound waves are created when objects vibrate. Fast vibrations produce high sounds, while slower vibrations produce lower sounds.

HOW SOUND TRAVELS

Sound waves can travel through air, water, or other materials. Some materials are better conductors of sound than others. Metals conduct sound very well, while soft materials like paper tend to muffle sound. When engineers, architects, and decorators are designing a space, they need to pay attention to how sound will work in that space–they study its acoustics. A concert hall or an auditorium will be designed to best transmit the sounds from the stage. Restaurants, by contrast, may want to use materials such as acoustic ceiling tiles that absorb sound so that people can converse easily.

THE SPEED OF SOUND

Sound travels at different speeds depending on the material it is traveling through. In air, sound travels more than 750 miles per hour (343 meters/second). In water, it moves even faster: more than 3,310 miles per hour (1,480 meters/second).

SOUND IN SPACE?

Sound can travel through different states of matter—solid, liquid, or gas. But it can't travel if there is no matter. Since space is a vacuum, sound doesn't travel through space.

VOCAL CORDS

How do humans create sound? One way to create sound is to speak. When you speak, you are using two folds of muscle tissue in your throat called vocal cords. When you breathe, your vocal cords are open. When you speak, they vibrate to create sound.

ORIGAMI POPPER

- Sheet of rectangular paper

We use construction paper here but you can use regular printer paper too.

Can paper make a noise louder than a quiet rustle? If you fold it the right way, it can.

Step 1

Fold the paper in half from top to bottom. Unfold it.

Step 2

Fold the paper in half from left to right. Unfold it.

Step 3

Fold one corner in towards the center of the origami model.

Step 4

Fold the other three corners in the same way.

Step 5

Rotate the model.

Step 6

Bring the top of the paper down along the center fold.

Step 7

Take the left corner. Fold it down at the center line. Do the same with the right corner.

Step 8

Flip the model over and rotate it as shown.

Step 9

Fold the model in half.

Step 10

If you hold it at one end, it should look like this.

Step 11

Hold the model by the points at the other end. Make sure you are not holding onto the interior folds.

Step 12

In a quick whipping motion, flick the model in the air. The interior folds will pop out, making a sound.

Step 13

If you don't get good results the first time, loosen the interior folds and try again.

LOUDSPEAKERS

Make loudspeakers for your smartphone with simple paper products.

MATERIALS

- Paper towels
- Paper towel roll
- Two paper cups
- Scissors
- Smartphone
- Pen

Step 1

Measure your phone against the paper towel roll and draw a slot where it will go.

Step 2

Cut a slot in the paper towel roll.

Step 3

The cups will go on either side of the paper towel roll.

Step 4

Draw a circle on each cup that matches the diameter of the paper towel roll.

Step 5

Cut holes in the paper cups.

Step 6

Crumple a paper towel into each end of the paper towel roll.

Step 7

Fit the cups to the paper towel roll.

Step 8

Fit your phone in the slot and play a song! What do you notice about the music? If you remove the paper towels, how does that affect the song?

FOR FURTHER TESTING

Try just putting your phone in a cup or bowl. Does that amplify or dampen the sound? Does it depend on the material? Try plastic, glass, and ceramic.

NOISY SPOONS

This simple experiment shows how well solid objects conduct sound.

MATERIALS

- Several metal spoons
- Yarn
- Scissors
- Tape

Step 1

Cut a length of yarn several feet long.

Step 2

Tape the spoons to the yarn. They should be close enough that the free ends of the spoons can clank together.

Step 3

The spoons clink and make noise.

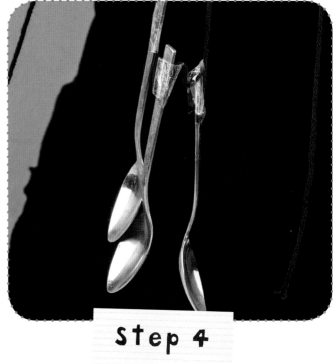

Step 4

Now hold the ends of the yarn up to your ears. Does it sound different? Do you think it sounds better or worse?

HOW DOES IT WORK?

The vibrations of the sound waves travel up the yarn to your ears. Because solid objects carry sound better than air, you will hear a difference in the quality of the sound.

FOR FURTHER FUN

Connect two paper cups to each other with a long length of string. Speak normally into the cup to a friend or sibling at the other end. How far apart can you get and still be heard?

MUSICAL INSTRUMENTS

Musical instruments have been around for a long time—flutes made of animal bones that date back 42,000 years have been found in Germany. Instruments are used for entertainment, rituals and religious services, and more. Music really is its own language and the many instruments can be used to convey countless different emotions.

The five major types of musical instruments are percussion, woodwind, stringed, brass and keyboard.

PERCUSSION

Percussion instruments are typically hit or shaken. These include drums that are hit with sticks (or with the hands), as well as tambourines or maracas which are shaken.

WOODWINDS

Woodwind instruments are made of wood and metal and get their sound from a person blowing air into or across the mouthpiece. A flute or a piccolo produces sound by blowing air across the edge on the side of the instrument. The other type of woodwinds use a reed, or thin piece of wood, to create sound when air vibrates the reed. The clarinet and saxophone have one reed, and the oboe and bassoon have two reeds, or a double reed.

STRINGED

Stringed instruments make sound by the vibration of strings. A guitar is a stringed instrument whose sound comes from the plucking of the strings with one's hand, fingers, or a pick. Other similarly played instruments include the harp, banjo, lute, and sitar. Another set of stringed instruments are played by moving a bow across the strings. The main bowed instruments are the violin, cello, and double bass.

BRASS

Brass instruments include the trumpet, tuba, trombone, French horn, bugle, and cornet. These brass instruments, like the woodwinds, require a mouthpiece and wind power from the mouth to push air through the instrument to vibrate and make sound.

KEYBOARD

Keyboard instruments are played with the hands. Pianos, organs, and harpsichords are examples of keyboard instruments.

Diatonic harmonicas play in a single key, often the key of C. Diatonic harmonicas are popular for beginners.

HARMONICAS

Harmonicas are a wind instrument. Harmonicas have several holes. Inside each hole is a reed. Players both blow air into and draw air from the harmonica to make noise. For instance, you might blow air in a hole to play one note, and draw air from that hole to play a note higher on the musical scale.

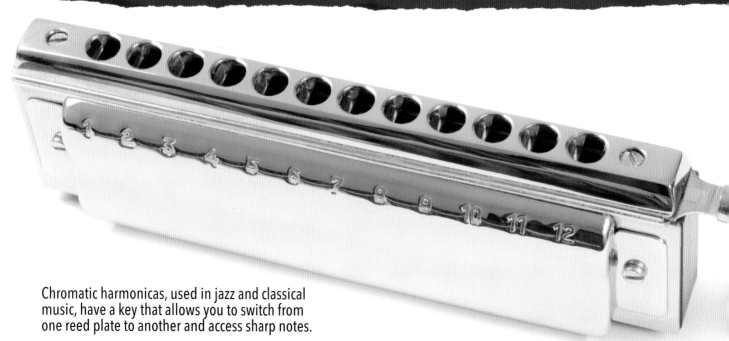

Chromatic harmonicas, used in jazz and classical music, have a key that allows you to switch from one reed plate to another and access sharp notes.

HARMONICA

Make your own harmonica and explore sound waves. How can you make different sounds?

MATERIALS

2 jumbo craft sticks

Wide rubber band

Plastic straw

Ruler

2 smaller rubber bands

Scissors

step 1

Stretch the wide rubber band lengthwise over one of the craft sticks.

step 2

Cut two pieces of straw, each 1–1½ inches (2½–3¾ cm) long.

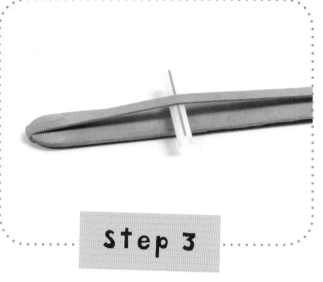

Step 3

Place one straw piece under the rubber band, about 2 inches (5 cm) from one end of the craft stick.

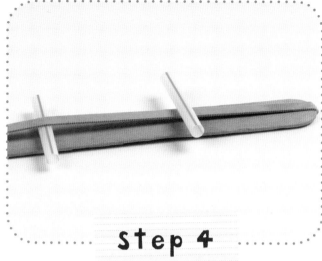

Step 4

Place the other straw piece on top of the rubber band, about 2 inches (5 cm) from the other end of the craft stick.

Step 5

Place the second craft stick on top of the first one, creating a sandwich with the straw pieces in the middle.

Step 6

Wrap a smaller rubber band about ½ inch (1¼ cm) from each end. To play your harmonica, put your mouth in the middle and blow through the sticks (not the straws). *Do you feel anything vibrating? Can you make different sounds by blowing through different areas, blowing harder or softer, or by moving the straws?*

HOW DOES IT WORK?

The sounds we hear are sound waves traveling through the air. Sound waves originate from a vibrating object, such as a vocal cord, and travel through the air. When you blow into your harmonica, you make the large rubber band vibrate, and that vibration produces sound. To change the pitch, slide the straws closer together or farther apart. When you slide the straws closer together, the section of rubber band that is vibrating is shorter, so it makes a higher sound.

GUITARS

Modern guitars have six strings. They have evolved over time from earlier instruments.

Lutes were used in medieval times and were popular in Renaissance music. A person who makes stringed instruments such as guitars is called a luthier, from the word "lute."

Acoustic guitars have a hollow chamber to project the sound.

Banjos, along with guitars, are classified as chordophones.

While classical guitars use strings made of gut or nylon, modern acoustic guitars use metal strings, as do electric guitars.

MAKE YOUR OWN GUITAR

Rubber bands form the strings on this DIY guitar.

MATERIALS

- Shoebox
- Paper towel tube
- Glue
- Scissors
- Rubber bands of varying thickness
- Compass

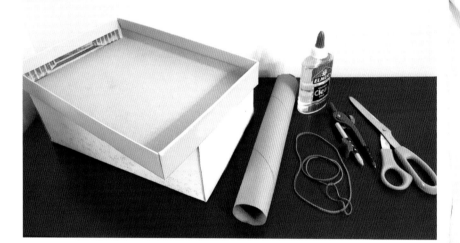

Step 1

Using the compass, draw a circle in the center of the lid of the shoebox.

Step 2

Ask an adult to score the circle with the tip of one blade of the scissors.

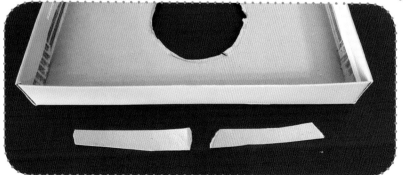

Step 3

Remove the circle from the shoebox lid. From it, cut out two narrow strips.

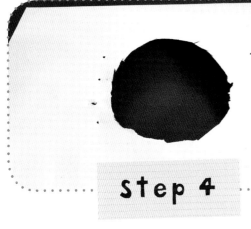

step 4

On either side of the center hole, carefully use the sharp tip of the compass to make four small holes.

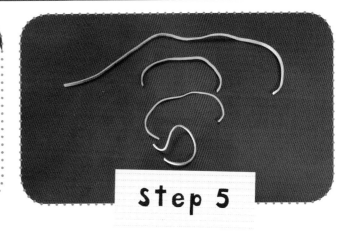

step 5

Cut each rubber band to make your strings.

step 6

Thread the rubber bands through the holes.

step 7

Tape down the rubber bands to the inside of the box.

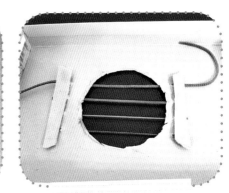

step 8

Glue down the strips of cardboard from step 3 to help keep the strings taut and in place.

step 9

Draw a circle around the cardboard tube on one end of the box and cut it out.

step 10

Fit the cardboard tube into the hole.

step 11

Place the lid on the box and try out your guitar!

You may have had a toy xylophone as a kid. But it and similar instruments can be used for serious music.

Concert xylophones have a range of several octaves.

XYLOPHONES

Xylophones are instruments in the percussion family. Mallets make sound waves when they strike bars, generally made of wood.

Marimbas come from the same musical family as xylophones.

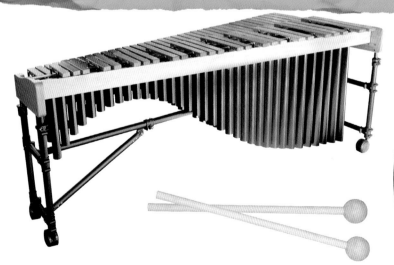

Xylophones used in orchestras have tubes beneath them. These tubes are called resonators, and they enhance the sound.

WATER GLASS XYLOPHONE

Create a symphony with water, glasses, and a spoon!

MATERIALS

- 8 glasses
- Water
- Food coloring (optional)
- Metal spoon
- Measuring cups

Step 1

Leave one glass empty. Fill the glass next to it with ¼ cup of water.

Step 2

Pour ½ cup in the third glass.

Step 3

Continue pouring water in each glass, increasing the amount by ¼ cup each time.

Glass 1: empty
Glass 2: ¼ cup
Glass 3: ½ cup
Glass 4: ¾ cup
Glass 5: 1 cup
Glass 6: 1 ¼ cup
Glass 7: 1 ½ cup
Glass 8: 1 ¾ cup

Step 4

Fill the glasses with different colors of food coloring if you'd like.

Step 5

Tap the glasses with the spoon to play a melody!

FOR FURTHER FUN

Try using spoons made of different materials. What material produces the best result? Pour the same amount of water in a short wide glass, a short thin glass, a tall wide glass, and a tall skinny glass. Do they produce the same pitch?

PIPES AND FLUTES

First made of animal bones and mammoth tusks, flutes have been used by humans for tens of hundreds of years. When a stream of air is directed across a hole in the flute, it creates a vibration of air that resonates through the hollow flute.

Pan flutes, also called panpipes, are often used in folk music. This set comes from Peru.

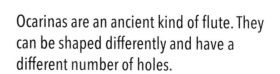

Ocarinas are an ancient kind of flute. They can be shaped differently and have a different number of holes.

STRAW PIPES

Create your own set of colorful panpipes
with straws.

MATERIALS

- 7 milkshake straws
- Clear tape
- Ruler
- Scissors

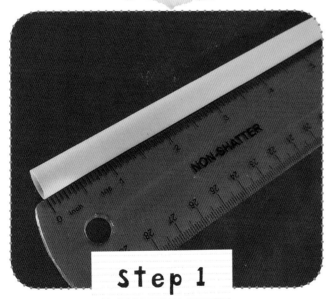

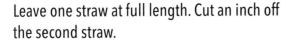

Step 1

Leave one straw at full length. Cut an inch off the second straw.

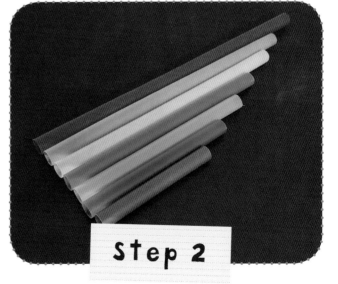

Step 2

Cut two inches off the third straw, three inches off the fourth straw, and so forth, until you have seven straws that vary by one inch in length.

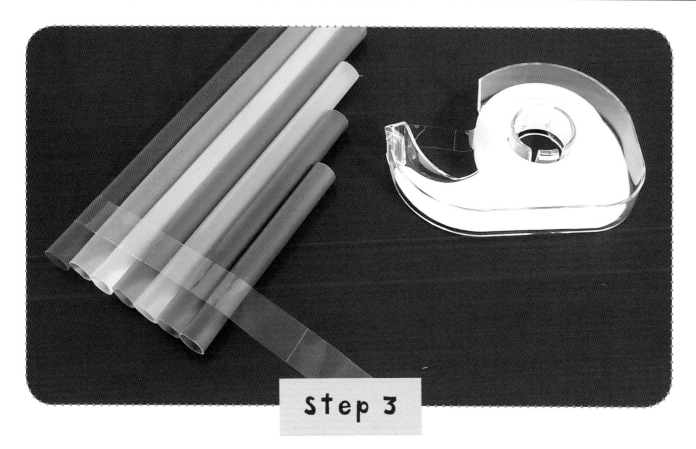

Step 3

Tape the straws on one side, then the other.

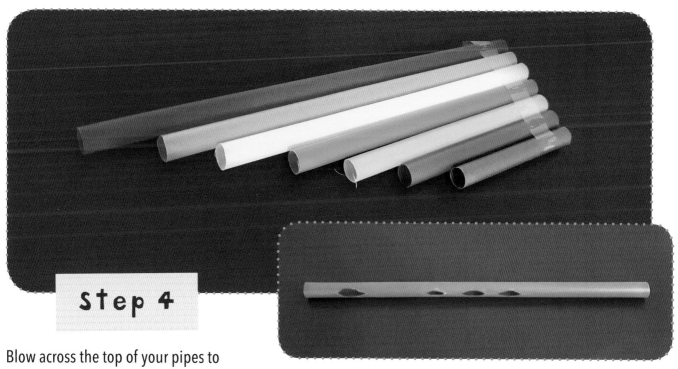

Step 4

Blow across the top of your pipes to make a light whistling noise. Do the longer or shorter straws produce the higher noise?

You can create a flute from a straw, too. Cut one hole to act as a mouth hole that you blow across. The other three holes act as finger holes. How does the pitch change when you cover one, two, or all three holes?

ELECTRICITY

When you turn on a light at home, or use a laptop, you're using electricity. But what is electricity? How do people harness it?

Electricity sounds similar to "electrons"–the negative particles found in atoms. There's a reason for that. In a neutral state, an atom has the same number of protons and electrons. The electrons are on the outside of the atom, with the protons on the inside. When atoms gain or lose electrons, it creates a charged state. If you have a group of atoms and their electrons are made to move from one atom to another, it creates electricity.

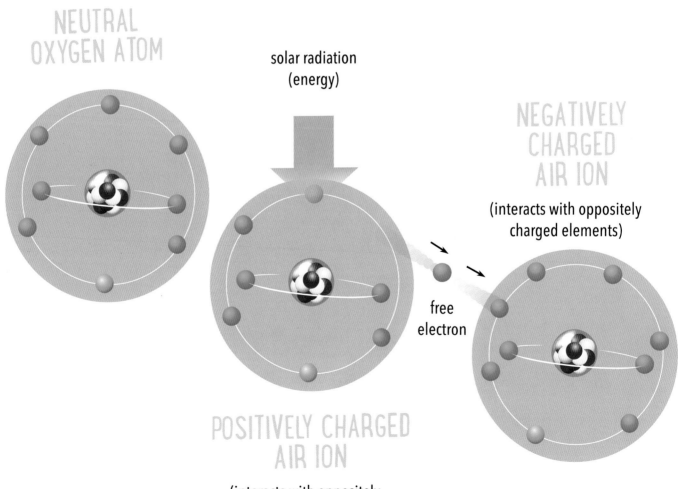

NEUTRAL
OXYGEN ATOM

solar radiation
(energy)

NEGATIVELY
CHARGED
AIR ION

(interacts with oppositely
charged elements)

free
electron

POSITIVELY CHARGED
AIR ION

(interacts with oppositely
charged elements)

CIRCUITS

An electric current moves through what is called a circuit. Let's say you turn on a light—when you click the switch, you are completing a circuit that allows the electric current to flow. Some materials such as metals are called conductors; they are very good at allowing electricity to flow through them. Other materials, called insulators, tend to slow down or halt an electric current.

LIGHTNING

Lightning is a form of electricity. Movement inside a thundercloud causes electrons to flow to the bottom of the cloud, while a positive charge of protons moves to the top. The negative charge tries to rejoin the positive charge by moving within a cloud, to another cloud, or to the ground. Lightning rods are made of conductive metal that can channel lightning safely to the ground.

Batteries store electric energy.

JUMPING LEAVES

Can you use the invisible forces of static electricity to make tissue paper leaves jump up without touching them?

MATERIALS

Balloon

Tissue paper

Something wool

Pencil

Scissors

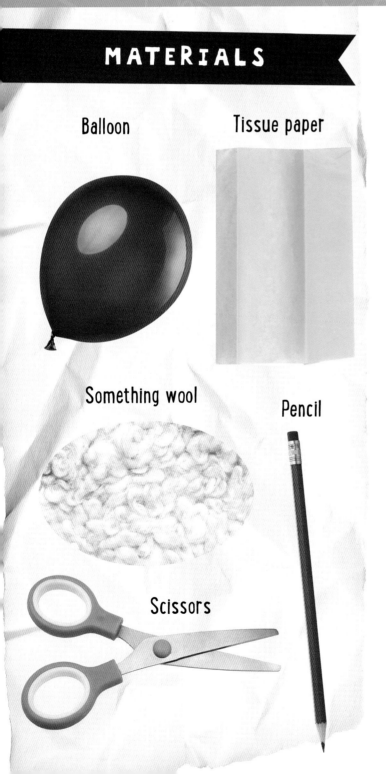

Step 1

Lay a single sheet of tissue paper flat on a table. Use a pencil to gently draw several leaves, each about 1½ inches (3.8 cm) long, onto the paper.

Step 2

Use scissors to carefully cut out the leaves. Place the cut-out leaves on a table.

Step 3

Inflate the balloon to its full size and tie off. Move the balloon a couple inches above the leaves. *Do you notice how nothing happens with the leaves?*

Step 4

Rub the balloon against something wool, such as a scarf or blanket, for about one minute. If you don't have anything wool, rub the balloon on your hair. The balloon is now electrically charged.

Step 5

Bring the charged balloon a few inches above the leaves and slowly move it closer. *What happens?* The leaves will be attracted to the balloon and eventually jump up toward it.

NOW TRY THIS!

Rub the balloon on wool as before. Bring the charged balloon close to a thin stream of running water. Watch the water bend toward the balloon.

HOW DOES IT WORK?

Static electricity is the buildup of electric charge in an object. Tiny particles called protons and electrons carry electric charge. Protons carry a positive (+) charge, and electrons carry a negative (-) charge. Objects that have opposite charges will attract, or pull together. Objects with the same charge will repel, or push apart. When you rub the balloon on wool, it picks up extra electrons, giving the balloon a negative charge. This pushes the electrons away in the paper, leaving a positive charge on the paper leaves. The negatively-charged balloon attracts the positively-charged paper leaves, causing them to jump up.

MAGNETS

Your refrigerator at home may be full of them, holding up to-do lists or artwork or just adding a splash of decorative fun. Have you ever wondered why magnets stick on a refrigerator door but not, say, on a wooden door?

OPPOSITES ATTRACT

Certain objects generate a magnetic field. In a magnetic field, all the electrons spin in the same direction. The Earth itself is a giant magnet that generates a magnetic field. Just like the Earth has a North and South Pole, where its magnetic fields are strongest, so do smaller magnets. Each small magnet has a "north" and "south" pole. If you touch two magnets to each other, they will attract each other when the north pole of one magnet comes near the south pole of the other. But if you touch the north pole of one magnet against the north pole of another, the two magnets will repel each other.

MAGNETIC MATERIALS

A mineral called magnetite-it's also called lodestone–is a natural magnet. People would use lodestone in compasses that pointed to the North Pole of the Earth. Iron and some other metals like nickel are ferromagnetic–they're strongly attracted to magnets, and can hold a magnetic field. While magnets do affect other materials such as paper or wood, the effect is so weak that it isn't noticeable.

MAKING A MAGNET

Iron and steel can be made into a magnet pretty easily. You can make a metal paper clip into a temporary magnet, for example, by rubbing a magnet against the paperclip many times, making sure to always rub in the same direction. Electromagnets are created when people run an electric field through a metal, creating a permanent magnet.

MAGNETS IN USE TODAY

Magnets are used in electric motors, to store data in computers, and in medical scanners. The strip of material on the back of a credit card is a magnetic strip that stores data codes.

FLY A KITE

You don't need a windy day to fly this construction-paper kite.

MATERIALS

- Construction paper
- Scissors
- Tape (or glue)
- Yarn or string
- Metal paper clip
- Magnet*

*Magnets are available at craft stores and hardware stores

Step 1

Cut out kite pieces from the construction paper.

Step 2

Cut a piece of yarn the length of the kite.

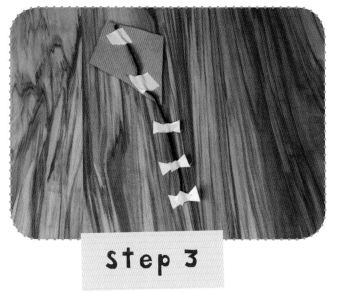

Step 3

Tape the yarn to the kite pieces. You can also use a dab of glue instead.

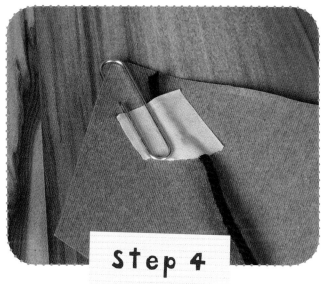

Step 4

Attach a metal paper clip to the top of the kite.

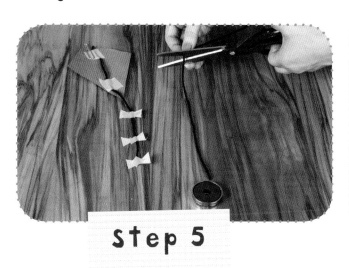

Step 5

For a circular magnet, thread your yarn through the hole in the magnet. For a bar magnet, use tape to attach the yarn to the magnet.

Step 6

When the magnet approaches the metal paper clip, it will lift the kite.

Step 7

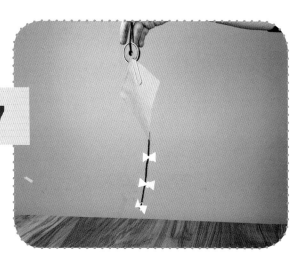

Fly your kite!

COMPASS

Which way is North? With this homemade compass, you'll always know the way.

MATERIALS

- Bowl
- Water
- Magnet*
- Needle (Metal)
- Cork*
- Scissors
- Tape
- Marker or pen

*You can often purchase magnets and cork at craft stores. Magnets are also found at hardware stores.

Step 1

Cut out a small piece of cork.

Step 2

Swipe the needle against the magnet at least 30 times, always in the same direction.

Step 3

Move the magnet away from your workspace. Tape the needle to the cork.

Step 4

Fill a bowl with water. Place your cork and needle in the bowl.

Step 5

The needle will point in a particular direction. You can verify by checking against a compass app on your smartphone that one end of the needle always points North.

Step 6

Mark "N" for North with a marker.

HOW DOES IT WORK?

In step 2, you are making the needle into a weak magnet. When it is close to the existing magnet, it will be attracted to it. But when the other magnet is moved away, the newly-magnetized needle then aligns itself with Earth's magnetic field.

SAFETY PIN CHAIN

Make paper clips or safety pins into weak magnets. How long can your chain get?

MATERIALS

- Safety pins or paper clips
- Two magnets

Step 1

Put up one magnet on the refrigerator. Magnetize a safety pin by swiping it against the other magnet 20 or 30 times, in the same direction. Then attach it to the magnet on the fridge.

Step 2

Magnetize more safety pins. Attach them carefully, one by one. How long can your chain get before gravity wins out?

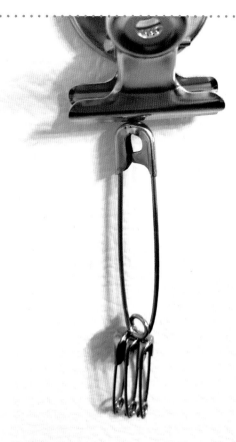

Step 3

You can also try to see how many safety pins you can attach to a single magnetized safety pin.

Step 4

What is your record? Can you start a second layer of safety pins?

GRAVITY

Gravity is a force that pulls matter together. Every object has gravity. You have gravity!

Objects with more matter have more gravity. Compared to you, the Earth has a much bigger gravitational pull. When you throw a ball in the air, it returns to the ground instead of floating in midair or bumping into you because of Earth's gravitational pull.

OUR MASSIVE SUN

The Sun has more mass than the Earth. The mass of the Sun is equivalent to the mass of 333,000 Earths. The Sun's gravitational pull keeps the Earth in orbit around it.

So if the Earth has less mass than the Sun, why does our Moon orbit the Earth instead of the Sun? It's because of distance. When an object is closer, it will exert a stronger gravitational pull. The Moon stays in orbit around the Earth because of Earth's gravitational pull. And the Moon exerts a gravitational pull on the Earth, too, that's reflected in the movement of the ocean tides.

Do **heavier** objects fall **faster?**

We know that objects fall towards the Earth because of gravity. Do objects with more mass fall faster to the ground? Let's turn the page and do an experiment to see.

BINDER CLIP VS. NAPKIN

A binder clip weighs more than a napkin. Will it fall faster? Let's see.

MATERIALS

- Three napkins
- Two binder clips

You can do this experiment with any objects you have around the house. Paper towels or printer paper can substitute for napkins, while pebbles or grapes can substitute for binder clips.

Step 1

Crumple up a napkin. Hold it and a binder clip or other small, dense object at the same height.

Step 2

Let them drop. What happens? They fall at the same speed. Gravity exerts the same force on both objects, regardless of mass.

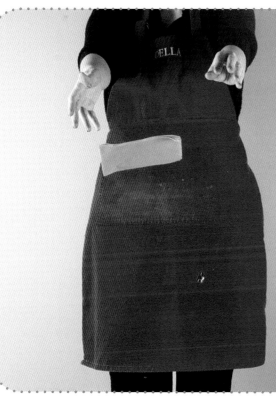

Step 3

Now let's see if we can introduce another element, that of air resistance. This time, use a napkin that is not crumpled.

While gravity pushes down on both objects, air resistance exerts a greater effect on the wide surface area of the napkin. It falls more slowly.

Step 4

You can create a makeshift parachute using a napkin and a second binder clip.

Step 5

The binder clip with the napkin "parachute" attached will fall more slowly than the binder clip by itself.

HOW DOES IT WORK?

Wide shapes such as parachutes maximize air resistance, countering the force of gravity.

PARACHUTES

When a skydiver jumps out of a plane, they immediately begin to fall. In the first part of a skydive, the freefall, the parachute is not yet deployed. The skydiver accelerates as they fall, eventually reaching a speed called terminal velocity. This is the greatest speed they will achieve. At this speed, the forces of gravity (weight) and its countering force drag (air resistance) balance each other out. Then the skydiver deploys the parachute to slow down their speed for a safe landing.

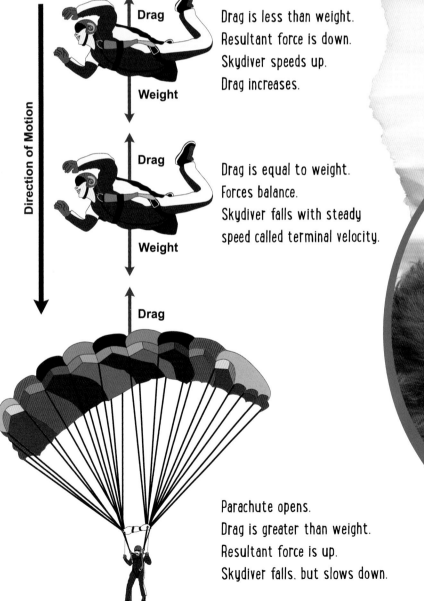

Direction of Motion

Drag

Weight

Drag is less than weight.
Resultant force is down.
Skydiver speeds up.
Drag increases.

Drag

Weight

Drag is equal to weight.
Forces balance.
Skydiver falls with steady speed called terminal velocity.

Drag

Parachute opens.
Drag is greater than weight.
Resultant force is up.
Skydiver falls, but slows down.

Weight

Because we can't see it, we often think of air as nothing. But air acts as a fluid, a substance that flows.

The shape of a parachute's canopy is carefully tailored to provide air resistance. Many parachutes today use a rectangular configuration known as a ram-air design. These are easier to control than traditional round chutes.

Many skydivers can work together to create incredible formations.

PAPER CUP PARACHUTE

Make a parachute and test it outdoors!

MATERIALS

- Plastic bag
- Scissors
- Paper cup
- Ribbon or yarn
- Small objects such as clothespins

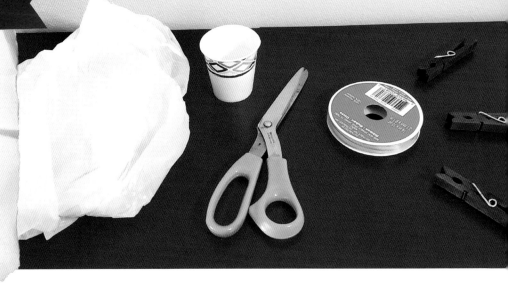

Step 1

Cut a square from the top of the plastic bag.

Step 2

Use the tips of the scissors to carefully poke four holes at the top of the cup, at equal distances from each other.

step 3

Cut four lengths of ribbon. Once you've cut one, you can measure the other three against that length of ribbon so they are all the same in length.

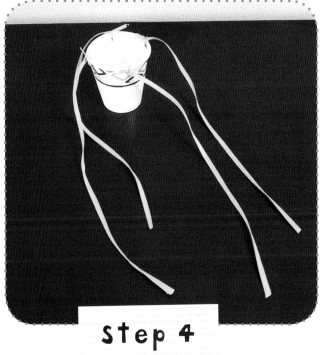

step 4

Thread each piece of ribbon through a hole in the cup. Knot it securely.

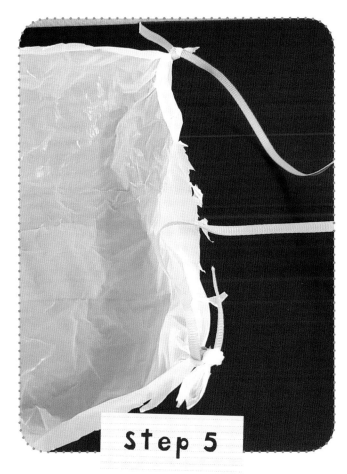

step 5

Secure each piece of ribbon to one corner of the plastic.

step 6

Drop your parachute from a balcony, second story window, or the top of a flight of steps to see how long it takes to reach the ground. Add small objects to see how much the parachute can carry. Take care not to drop your parachute on anything underneath.

Sculptors have to address practical issues when carrying out their creative vision. They need to make sure that things are balanced and strong, and that the sculpture has the support it needs.

STRONG SHAPES

Every new structure begins with a plan. Engines and machines are worked on by mechanical engineers. Civil engineers work on structures such as dams, bridges, and canals. Architects design houses and skyscrapers, working with a team of other specialists such as electrical and structural engineers. These professionals study shapes and materials. How can the structures they build best withstand forces such as wind, earthquakes, and time?

Today, most new houses in the United States have air conditioning. But air conditioning has only been around for about a century. Before that time, builders in areas that got hot in the summer had several strategies, such as shaded windows, for circulating air and staying cool.

Some civil engineers specialize in making sure buildings can stand against earthquakes.

Available materials often affect shapes and structures. When pioneers were settling the Great Plains, they did not always have wood to build houses. Instead, they used sod, a combination of grass and soil.

CRAFT STICK TRUSSES

Buildings and bridges are usually supported by a truss, a framework of beams or bars that are connected at their ends. An engineer's goal is to design a truss that won't bend or break. Find out what geometric shape forms the strongest truss in this experiment.

MATERIALS

7 jumbo craft sticks

7 small binder clips

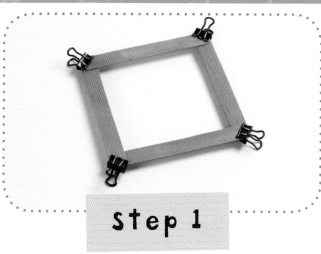

Step 1

Make a square with 4 craft sticks. Join the ends with a small binder clip at each corner.

Step 2

Grip 2 adjacent craft sticks and gently try to rotate them. *How easy is it to rotate the craft sticks?*

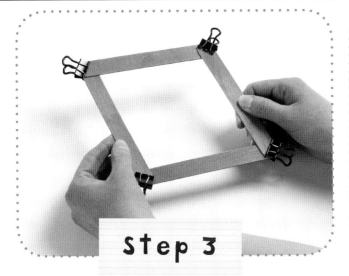

Step 3

Grip 2 craft sticks on opposite sides of the square and gently try to slide them back and forth parallel to each other. *How easy is it to slide the craft sticks? What happens to the shape of the square?*

Step 4

Now make a triangle with 3 craft sticks. Join the ends with small binder clips.

IN REAL LIFE!

See how triangles work in a real life bridge!

Step 5

Grip 2 adjacent craft sticks and gently try to rotate them just like you did with the square. Try sliding the craft sticks back and forth. *How does the triangle compare with the square? Which shape makes the stronger truss?*

HOW DOES IT WORK?

You probably found that it was easy to rotate and slide the sticks in your square truss. Your square might have even turned into a parallelogram. But you probably couldn't rotate or slide the sticks in your triangle truss. That's because a triangle is a rigid shape. Structures built with triangles are much stronger than those built with only squares.

BRIDGES

The concept of a bridge is simple—a span you can walk or drive across in order to get to the other side. But bridges present complicated engineering challenges. How can a long bridge be supported? How can the bridge work with the wind? How can you keep the bridge strong throughout the length of its span? Different types of bridges are used to address different situations. Here are some of the most common types.

Beam bridges have a very simple structure, consisting of a span supported on either end. Some beam bridges can have multiple spans, supported by piers underneath. Beam bridges tend to be shorter in length.

Truss bridges use the strong triangular shape to distribute stresses.

Arch bridges are supported by abutments at each end.

San Francisco's Golden Gate Bridge is an iconic suspension bridge. Vertical suspension cables connect to the main cables, which in turn connect to the ground on either side of the bridge and to the towers at intervals.

Cable-stay bridges have towers with cables that connect to the deck in order to support it. This bridge, Guadina Bridge, links the countries of Portugal and Spain.

CRAFT STICK BRIDGE

Build your own truss bridge!

MATERIALS

- Craft sticks
- Wood glue
- Paper towels or newspapers to protect surfaces from glue

Step 1

Lay out the sides of the bottom of your bridge using 4 overlapping craft sticks on each side. Use dabs of glue to join them together.

Step 2

Fill in the bottom of your bridge with craft sticks acting as planks. Set the bottom aside to dry completely.

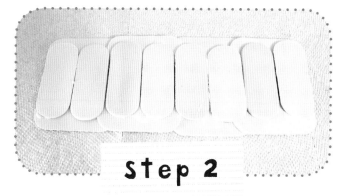

Step 3

The sides of your bridge will be formed with triangles. Begin with one triangle.

Step 4

Create a second triangle that overlaps the first.

Step 5

The side should be as long as the bottom of the bridge.

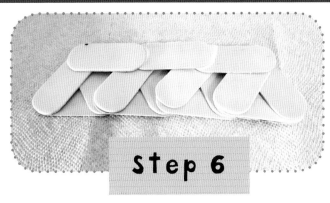

Step 6

Add craft sticks to form the top of the side. Set the piece aside to dry completely.

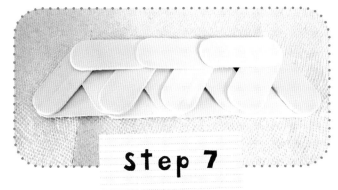

Step 7

Create the second side of the bridge. Set the piece aside to dry completely.

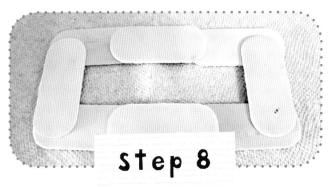

Step 8

Create a rectangle of craft sticks to form the top of the bridge.

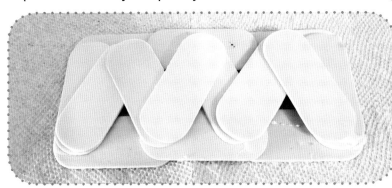

Step 9

Strengthen the top by filling it in with triangles. Set the piece aside to dry completely.

Step 10

When all sides of the bridge have dried and the glue has set, glue one side to the bottom.

Step 11

Glue the other side to the bottom. Prop the sides in place to dry completely.

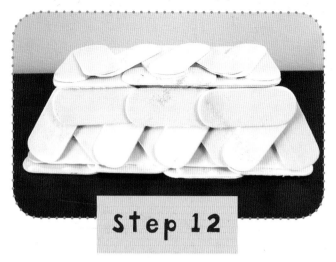

Step 12

Glue the top to the piece.

Step 13

Let the piece dry completely overnight.

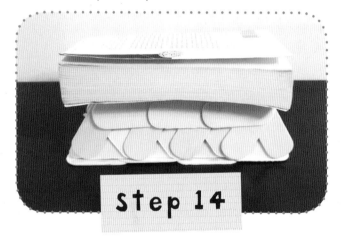

Step 14

Test your bridge. How much weight can it take?

Step 15

Use books and add them one by one.

Step 16

Your bridge might carry more weight than you expect!

Step 17

When the bridge cracks, weigh the books on a scale. See how much weight your bridge carried. Try different designs to see if that affects how much weight the bridge carries!